PRIMARY SOURCES OF EVERYDAY LIFE IN COLONIAL AMERICA™

Government and Politics in Colonial America

Charlie Samuel

The Rosen Publishing Group's
PowerKids Press™
New York

Published in 2003 by The Rosen Publishing Group, Inc.
29 East 21st Street, New York, NY 10010

First Edition

Photo Credits: Key: t: top, b: below, c: center, l: left, r: right
p. 4 Corbis/Bettmann; p.4tr Corbis/Library of Congress; p.7tr Bridgeman Art Library/ Museum of the City of New York; pp.7cr & b, 8tr Corbis/Bettmann; p.8tr Corbis/Lee Snider; p.11br Bridgeman Art Library/John Noot Gallery, Broadway, Worcester; p.11cl Bridgeman Art Library/Middle Temple , London; pp.11tl, 12tr, 15b Peter Newark's American Pictures; p.15cr Bridgeman Art Library/Museum of Fine Arts, Boston; p.16b Corbis/Bettmann; p.16tl Hulton Archive; pp.16tr, 19bl & t Peter Newark's American Pictures; p.20cl Bridgeman Art Library.

Library of Congress Cataloging-in-Publication Data

Samuel, Charlie.
  Government and politics in colonial America / Charlie Samuel.
      v. cm. – (Primary sources of everyday life in colonial America)
Includes bibliographical references and index.
Contents: The race for colonies – Setting up colonial governments – Royal colonies – Charter colonies – Proprietary colonies – Politics among the colonies – Colonial politicians – Debates and documents – Revolutionary politics – Colonial foundations of democracy.
  ISBN 0-8239-6597-X (library binding)
  1. United States–Politics and government–To 1775–Juvenile literature. 2. United States–Politics and government–To 1775–Sources–Juvenile literature. [1. United States–Politics and government–To 1775.] I. Title. II. Series.
  E188 .S19 2003
  325'.341'0973–dc21

                                        2002004469

Contents

The 13 English colonies were:

Connecticut
Delaware
Georgia
Maryland
Massachusetts
New Hampshire
New Jersey
New York
North Carolina
Pennsylvania
Rhode Island
South Carolina
Virginia

▲ England claimed the area colored in yellow on this map. The green area shows land claimed by the French. They both wanted the pink area.

◄ The Pilgrims claimed Plymouth Colony for England in 1620.

The Race for the Colonies

After Europeans discovered America late in the fifteenth century, countries raced to claim the best land there. They took the land as if no one lived there, even though it was home to many Native Americans. Some Native Americans were hostile because they thought the settlers would take their land. Others were friendly and showed settlers how to grow crops. The Europeans set up communities called **colonies** in places that they thought would be good for farming.

The Spanish began colonies in Mexico and South America. In 1607, the English started the first colonies on the east coast of North America. The French claimed the land to the north, which is now Canada, and later the land west of the Mississippi River, including present-day Louisiana. The Dutch and Swedish also had small colonies.

The English colonies grew quickest. By 1669, the English claimed all of the coast, from New England in the North to Georgia in the South. In all they had 13 colonies.

Setting up Colonial Governments

At first, colonists had to obey English laws and pay money to the English government. The colonies were a long way from England, however. The English gave each colony its own government to run the colony's affairs.

Colonies had different kinds of governments, royal, charter, or **proprietary**. The English king sent **governors** to run some colonies on his behalf. Colonies with appointed governors were called royal colonies. The king also granted **charters** to allow companies or individuals to set up their own colonies, called charter colonies. If one man had a charter, the colony was called a proprietary colony.

Colonial governors were helped by councils of advisers. In most colonies, male colonists also voted for a group of **freemen** to sit in an **assembly**. The freemen told the colonies' leaders what the colonists thought about colonial affairs. The colonists did not always agree with English laws and ideas.

This was New Amsterdam's statehouse in 1642. Under English rule, the town name was changed to New York.

This woodcut shows the first assembly at Jamestown in 1619.

Before there were newspapers, people heard the decisions of the government from town criers. A drummer let people know that the town crier had arrived.

► The Rhode Island assembly met at the White Horse Tavern from 1673 to 1687.

▼ In 1685, the English king sent an official to Connecticut to revoke its charter. The charter vanished. Some people say it was hidden in a tree.

Charter Colonies

Some of the first colonies were charter colonies. Companies of **investors** would pay to set up a colony. They hoped to find gold, to trade furs, or to sell land. A share of company profits went to the English king. Charters gave companies the right to set up any kind of government. A royal council made sure that the companies were governing the colonies well.

The first charter colony was Virginia. The Virginia Company began the settlement in 1607, at Jamestown. The company appointed leaders to run the colony. The colonists also voted for **burgesses**. Twice per year, the burgesses met in an assembly to discuss the new laws made by the company in London. The assembly could reject these laws. The colonists needed laws that worked for life in Virginia, not laws that worked for life in England.

By 1624, the Virginia Company had no money left. King James ended the company's charter and Virginia became a royal colony.

Proprietary Colonies

Individuals with royal charters set up proprietary colonies. The proprietors were often English nobles. The proprietor of New York, for example, was James, duke of York, who was the brother of King Charles II. James took New Netherland from the Dutch in 1664 to start his colony.

Proprietors ran their colonies as if the colonies were their own possessions. They decided what form of government to create. Usually, colonists could vote for an assembly to advise the proprietors. The proprietors and their officials ran the colony, though. The Calvert family, for example, ran Maryland for nearly 150 years after it was granted to George Calvert in 1632.

Proprietors could make laws that were different from English laws. William Penn founded Pennsylvania in 1681. Penn was a **Quaker**. He allowed colonists in Pennsylvania to choose their own religion and to worship in the way that they wanted. In England, the government made people follow the Protestant faith.

► George Calvert was also called Lord Baltimore. The main town in the colony of Maryland was named Baltimore for him.

◄ Sir Peter Lely was one of the eight proprietors who started a colony in Carolina in 1663. In 1691, the colony split into North and South Carolina.

► In this painting, William Penn receives a charter from King Charles II in 1681. Penn started the colony of Pennsylvania.

▶ This seal belonged to the Massachusetts Bay Company. King Charles II made Massachusetts a royal colony in 1684, after the colony tried to become independent.

▼ Sir George Carteret landed in New Jersey in 1664. He was the first governor of the colony after the English took it from the Dutch.

Royal Colonies

A royal colony was controlled by a governor on behalf of the English king. When the English first began moving to America in the seventeenth century, the king granted charters to companies and to individuals to begin settling. When the colonies grew wealthy, the king wanted to take control of them. By the early eighteenth century, the king had taken many of the colonies under royal control, including Virginia, New York, and Massachusetts.

In royal colonies, power lay with a governor. He had the only key to the box where the great seal was locked. A new law could not become official until it was stamped with this seal. The governor could give out land to settlers. He told them where they could hold markets, when to go to church, and how to behave. The governor was also in charge of the **militia**.

The English government appointed a council of officials in the colony to advise and help the governor. The council often included law officers.

Politics Among the Colonies

The English still had a lot of power in the colonies' governments. Colonists were angry when King James II created the Dominion of New England in 1686. The king forced six colonies to join together against their will. When James was forced off the throne in 1688, the colonists ended the Dominion.

By 1691, every colony had an assembly of freemen. Only men who owned land could vote. Women could not vote, and neither could Native Americans or any black Americans. Even so, a greater share of people could vote in the colonies than could vote in England at the time.

The assemblies could refuse to support English laws that did not help the colonies. The English government gave colonial governors the right to dismiss an assembly or to refuse to sign the laws that assemblies made. Colonists believed that assemblies should have the same status as Parliament had in England. Parliament could not be dismissed unless Parliament itself agreed.

▼ Governor Edmund Andros of New York reads the order that created the Dominion of New England in 1686.

▶ Samuel Adams was an important eighteenth-century politician who shared his ideas by writing letters to other colonial politicians.

George Mason was a leading politician in Virginia. He urged the 13 colonies to work together to end English rule.

William Penn wrote this book about the government in his colony, Pennsylvania. His ideas shaped the laws of the colony.

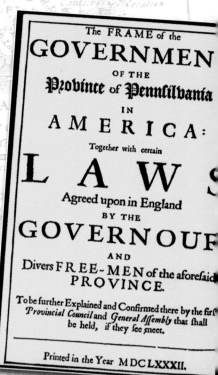

The FRAME of the
GOVERNMEN
OF THE
Province of Pennsilvania
IN
AMERICA:
Together with certain
LAWS
Agreed upon in England
BY THE
GOVERNOUR
AND
Divers FREE-MEN of the aforesaid
PROVINCE.

To be further Explained and Confirmed there by the first Provincial Council and General Assembly that shall be held, if they see meet.

Printed in the Year MDCLXXXII.

James Oglethorpe shakes hands with the Creek leader, Tomochichi, in 1733. The Creek let Oglethorpe start the colony of Georgia on the Savannah River.

Colonial Politicians

At first, colonial leaders usually came from England. This was still true after England joined with Scotland to create Great Britain in 1707. The leaders were wealthy and from the upper classes in society. One such leader was James Oglethorpe, who became the first governor of Georgia in 1732. Oglethorpe thought that America was a good place to try to create a society that would be fairer and more religious than the society in Europe. He banned slavery and stopped people from drinking beer and other kinds of alcohol. The colonists in Georgia soon overturned Oglethorpe's bans.

As the colonies grew, a new sort of politician became more common. These men were still wealthy. What made them different was that they were American, not English. Many had never even been to England. They had ideas about how to make America different from England. Some did not think that America should have a king at all.

Debates and Documents

To spread their ideas farther, colonists often wrote them down. Letters and documents were easy to send to other colonies, and even to Great Britain. Printers were highly respected. The famous politician and inventor Benjamin Franklin was a printer.

One important debate was about whether or not Britain should still govern the colonies. Many colonists thought that the colonies should govern themselves. Another debate was about religion. Colonies such as Massachusetts began as homes for followers of one faith or another. Now many colonists did not want the church to be part of the government at all.

Slavery was also a subject of debate. Many colonists were against slavery. Slaves were important workers, though, especially in Georgia and the Carolinas. Those colonies relied on slaves to work on **plantations**. Even some politicians who wrote or spoke out against slavery owned slaves themselves.

▼ *This painting shows politicians arriving at the Constitutional Convention in 1787. The convention decided the kind of government the United States would have.*

▶ *The Articles of Confederation served as America's constitution between 1781 and 1789. It listed the basic laws or rules that the states needed to follow.*

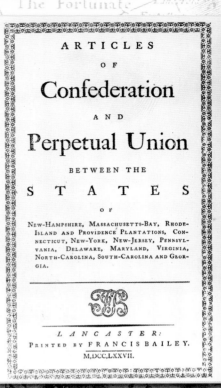

ARTICLES
OF
Confederation
AND
Perpetual Union
BETWEEN THE
STATES
OF
NEW-HAMPSHIRE, MASSACHUSETTS-BAY, RHODE-ISLAND AND PROVIDENCE PLANTATIONS, CONNECTICUT, NEW-YORK, NEW-JERSEY, PENNSYLVANIA, DELAWARE, MARYLAND, VIRGINIA, NORTH-CAROLINA, SOUTH-CAROLINA AND GEORGIA.

LANCASTER:
PRINTED BY FRANCIS BAILEY.
M,DCC,LXXVII.

A
DIALOGUE,
CONCERNING THE
SLAVERY
OF THE
AFRICANS;
Shewing it to be the *Duty* and *Interest* of the *American* Colonies to emancipate all their *African* Slaves:

WITH AN
ADDRESS to the Owners of such Slaves.

DEDICATED TO THE HONORABLE THE
Continental Congress.

Open thy mouth, judge righteously, and plead the cause of the poor and needy — PROV. XXXI. 9.
And as ye would that men should do to you, do ye also to them likewise. — LUKE VI 31.

NORWICH:
Printed and sold by JUDAH P. SPOONER. 1776.

▲ At this meeting of the assembly in Virginia, a man named Patrick Henry said, "Give me liberty or give me death," meaning he would rather die than be ruled by the British.

▶ This is the Declaration of Independence, which made the United States a free country. It was written on animal skin called parchment, so that it would last.

▶ King George of England issued this document to say that the American colonies were rising up against Britain and were a threat to British rule.

By the KING,

A PROCLAMATION,

For suppressing Rebellion and Sedition.

GEORGE R.

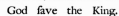

God save the King.

Revolutionary Politics

By the 1760s, many colonial politicians said that they no longer wanted to obey the British. Things were now very different from when the colonies first began. They had their own leaders, their own laws, their own churches and schools, and their own ideas. The people thought of themselves as being American, not British.

The British made the colonists pay taxes. However, they would not let the colonists take part in the British government, which made the tax laws. Some colonial leaders, such as Thomas Jefferson, George Washington, and Samuel Adams, began to have revolutionary ideas about making the colonies independent from Britain.

In 1765, colonists rejected a tax on paper. The English sent soldiers to collect taxes on other goods. In April 1775, fighting broke out between English troops and American militia. This was the start of the American Revolution, which lasted eight years. The colonies won and formed the United States of America in 1787.

Colonial Foundations of Democracy

In May 1789, Americans met in Philadelphia to set up a new government for the United States. The 13 colonies had become states in the new country. Apart from Rhode Island, all the states sent politicians to the meeting.

The politicians decided that they would not be ruled by a king, as were the British. Americans would elect a president to lead the nation. To stop the president from being too powerful, the people would also elect a Congress. The Congress would consist of senators and representatives. As colonial assemblies had done, Congress would represent the voice of the people. Americans still vote to choose the president, senate, and house of representatives.

Today all Americans have the right to vote. That was not true in 1789. Women were not allowed to vote. Black Americans and Native Americans were also left out of politics. America had only taken the first steps toward **democracy**.

Glossary

assembly (uh-SEM-blee) A group of people who meet to advise a government.

burgesses (BUR-jis-is) Citizens elected to help rule colonial Virginia.

charters (CHAR-turz) Written documents that allow an area to be used but not owned.

colonies (KAH-luh-neez) New places where people live, but where they are still ruled by their old country's leaders.

democracy (dih-MAH-kruh-see) A government that is run by the people who live under it.

freemen (FREE-muhn) Men who are not slaves or servants.

governors (GUH-vuh-nurz) Officials who are put in charge of a colony by a king or queen.

investors (in-VES-turz) People who give money for something they hope will bring them more money later.

militia (muh-LIH-shuh) A group of people who are trained and ready to fight in an emergency.

plantations (plan-TAY-shunz) Very large farms where crops like tobacco were grown.

proprietary (pruh-PRY-uh-ter-ee) Belonging to an individual owner.

Quaker (KWAY-kur) A person who follows a religion that believes in equality for all people, stong families and communities, and peace.

Index

Primary Sources

Page 4 (top). *Carte des Possessions Angloises et Francoises du Continent de l'Amerique Septentrionale* by Jean Palairet, 1755. **Page 7 (top).** The Stadt Huys of New York, at the corner of Pearl Street and Coentje Slip, is a lithograph in the possession of the New York Historical Society. **Page 8 (top).** Photograph of restored White Horse Tavern, Newport, Rhode Island. **Page 11 (top right).** The portrait of George Calvert was painted by Daniel Mytens the Elder, who was the official painter of King James I and King Charles I. **Page 12 (top).** The Seal of the Massachusetts Bay Company features a Native American who is saying "Come Over and Help Us." **Page 15 (inset).** Portrait of Samuel Adams painted by John Singleton Copley, probably between 1770 and 1772. Adams holds a scroll that demands that British troops be removed from Boston, and points to the charter of the Massachusetts colony with his other hand. The portrait is owned by the Museum of Fine Arts in Boston. **Page 16 (top left).** George Mason commissioned a portrait of himself from John Hesselius of Annapolis, Maryland. Later, Mason's son had three copies made of the original painting by D. W. Boudet. **Page 16 (top right).** Title page of *The Frame of the Government of the Province of Pennsylvania*, dated 1682. **Page 19 (top right).** *The Articles of Confederation*, printed in 1777. **Page 19 (bottom left).** Antislavery pamphlet printed in 1776 to ask the Continental Congress to end slavery. **Page 20 (center left).** The final draft of the Declaration of Independence, parchment, 1776. **Page 20 (bottom right).** Royal proclamation by King George III, printed in London in 1775.

Web Sites

Due to the changing nature of Internet links, PowerKids Press has developed an online list of Web sites related to the subject of this book. This site is updated regularly. Please use this link to access the list: www.powerkidslinks.com/pselca/gpca